A METHOD TO FACILITATE THE ACQUISITION OF VIRTUES THROUGH THE PARTICULAR EXAM

By Fr. Mariano José de Ibargüengoitia.

REVISED EDITION 2020

The Particular Exam.

By Fr. Mariano José de Ibargüengoitia y Zuloaga

Edition revised, corrected and translated of the 1st edition "Método para facilitar la adquisición de las virtudes por medio del examen particular, por el Presbítero Mariano José de Ibargüengoitia" printed in México in 1855 by Imprenta de Abadiano.

2020

"Your particular examination should be directed towards the acquisition of a definite virtue or the rooting out of your predominant defect."

"The general examination implies defense. The particular, attack. The first is your armor. The second, your sword."

San Josemaría Escrivá. The Way 241, 238.

Prologue to the present edition

The author of this book, the priest Mariano José de Ibargüengoitia y Zuloaga, is one of the many Spanish founders who have left their mark on the Catholic Church. He was born in Bilbao on September 8, 1815, the same year in which Saint John Bosco was born and with whom he also shares the same date of death: January 31, 1888. Between both dates, he received priestly ordination at the Roman basilica of San Juan de Letrán on April 18, 1840.

During his priestly life, he promoted the foundation of different religious communities. In 1857 he promoted the arrival in Bilbao of the nuns of Our Lady of Refuge, for the rehabilitation of women who had fallen into prostitution. Two years later, he promoted the coming to the same city of the Sisters of the Cross. In 1871, he collaborated in the foundation of the Carmelite College of Charity in Zumaya (Guipúzcoa), in 1878 he called the same nuns to open another school in Deusto and in 1879 he helped the Passionists to settle in the town.

From 1871 he collaborated decisively with Saint María Josefa del Corazón de Jesús (1842-1912) in the foundation of the

Congregation of the Servants of Jesus of Charity, being the spiritual director of it.

Culminating a priestly life of dedication to God and to the brothers, he died with the reputation of holiness on January 31, 1888 in Bilbao. On July 10, 2020, Pope Francis approved the decree of Heroic Virtues of the Servant of God by which he is considered "Venerable", an important step on the path of his cause for canonization.

In 1858 he published in two volumes his best-known work the "Spiritual Exercises for Priests", whose full title is "Exercises of Saint Ignatius of Loyola adapted exclusively to the spiritual use of the priests" according to the method of Saint Ignatius of Loyola, a book recommended by Archbishop Saint Anthony María Claret, who said that "it should be in every priestly library". In fact it appears in the short list of the private library of Saint Josemaría Escrivá in Rome. Two editions of it were published: that of Madrid, in 1857 with printing and writing of *La Regeneración*: two volumes of 300 pages and 372 respectively. A Second Edition, "augmented with an appendix containing exams" was published in 1880 in Barcelona, by *Librería Religiosa.*

A good proof of the spiritual finesse of Ibargüengoitia is also the work you have in your hands "Method to facilitate the acquisition of the virtues through the particular exam." The first and only edition so far was printed in Mexico in 1855, (First Edition "With the Necessary Licenses." Mexico, Abadiano Press, Calle 1a de Santo Domingo, No. 12), so it seemed appropriate to dust it off and make it available to the general public through a new updated edition available also in digital format.

For this edition I have tried to be as faithful as possible to the original, adapting first the syntax to the current Spanish before translating it into American English. I have to thank Jorge   J.

Rodriguez-Florido for his invaluable assistance editing this English version.

The content has also been slightly altered, moving to the end of the book as Annexes two portions that seem less useful to the average reader and that interrupted the structure of the original book. One is the detailed schedule suggested for doing spiritual exercises, which I understand will be rather the responsibility of the organizers of them. The other is a set of tables designed to keep track of misdemeanors, so meticulous that may induce scruples and that, in any case, seem somewhat superfluous in this digital age.

Bart M. Mariner

Editor & Publisher

Introduction

How happy is the soul that seeking by all means the will of the Lord, does not nourish in their heart another desire than that of fulfilling it with exactitude! What peace, what tranquility and how happy God makes them savor even in the midst of the hardships of life! Intimately convinced of the false brilliance of human greatness, they expect solid goods to the utmost degree, generously despising the flattery of a world that cannot fully satisfy the desires of the heart; and just as the soft fragrance of the fresh flowers makes itself felt more and more by those who come closer to a pleasant garden, so the scent of heavenly delights gives, even in this life, to the faithful soul who with the practice of virtue goes walking to the garden of his eternal happiness. Lucky luck, and how little known you are!

But great advantages are not achieved without some sacrifices. When man lived in the state of innocence, he did good without difficulty. The understanding and the will were rectified and whole to carry out their own acts, and the lower part was entirely subject to reason. But now that the natural, that the passions, that the devil, that our very fellow beings are impelling us towards evil, it is necessary to strive to sustain oneself, and to be brave enough to overcome the desires of our appetites.

It is true that God, rich in mercy, feeling sorry for our great evils, gives us a robust grace, with which we can take from us all vices, and plant in their place all the virtues; but this same God wants the triumph of this grace to be also the work of our endeavors, our study and our constant care in examining our actions to rectify, improve and perfect them.

The apostolic Fathers have regarded the examination of conscience as one of the most important means of advancing on the path of virtue. Saint Basil, Saint Augustine, Saint Bernard, Saint Bonaventure and others have entrusted us of doing it once or twice each day; and Saint Ignatius of Loyola made so much appreciation of this exercise, that in a certain way he preferred it to that of prayer.

Even the pagan philosophers without any other guide than natural reason, knew how to understand the importance of this medium. Among the documents that Pythagoras gave to his disciples, one was that each one had two times indicated every day, one in the morning and the other at night, to examine themselves and take into account these three things: what did I do? How I did it? And what I stopped doing what I should have done? Seneca, Plutarch and others recommend the same.

But the apostolic Fathers were not content with just advising the practice of the general examination. A long experience and their deep knowledge of our weakness and misery have unveiled the need to add the particular exam to the general examination, and I believe I do good to souls, desirous as I am of their eternal health, explaining to them in this booklet, what is this examination, its importance, and all things that to the effect it is convenient to know.

This instruction may be equally useful to people living in retirement in the cloister, as to those who are in the middle of the world, because to one and the other it has been said: *Be perfect, as is your heavenly Father*[1], and to that end this medium is very appropriate and easy to put it all into practice. May the Lord inspire those who read it the ardent desire to take advantage of it to better secure their future outcome, sweeten the bitterness of the present, and also get infused on the heavenly delights that his divine goodness often gives to souls who continuously serve him faithfully.

---

[1] Mt 5, 48

I. The Particular Exam. Definition and importance

The particular examination is nothing other than the scrutiny that we make of our defects on a matter in which we have specially proposed to reform. Thus, just as in the general examination, we compare our actions with all the obligations we have towards God, towards our neighbor and towards ourselves, deducting from this comparison the sins and faults that our souls are stained with. In particular, we compare our actions with only one of these duties to know the defects that we have committed against it.

By this means so easy and simple, the soul puts into action all the forces that grace is communicating to it in the holy Sacraments, in prayer and in other exercises of virtue that are supposed to be practiced to arrive to perfection. They scrutinize their faults, look once and over again, compare them with those of the previous days, recognizing the differences; and being attentive to the reasons that have caused the advances or the delays. They prepare to improve from now on with the resources that the experience of the past has provided.

It is true that also the general examination practiced daily, is destined to produce the same effect, and even better, and that for that very reason the practice of that one is not enough cause to never omit this one; but nevertheless, it is necessary to admit that for many people, the general examination is both sterile and unsuccessful, recessing into a mere memory of one's actions, which facilitates the prior disposition that they must have to manifest their guilt in the sacrament of confession.

This particular exam exercise also comforts and encourages souls who begin to serve God. In those first moments of fervor with which a soul enters to serve God, when it is still very little aware of its misery, and very proud of its own strength, it wish, and it seems to it that instead of walking, it runs to the highest of perfection; but when meeting head-on with a multitude of little fondnesses, with small inclinations and faults that embarrass its march, it becomes frightened and disconsolate, not having enough patience to wait for time to make the progress of his spirit palpable.

For the practice of the particular examination facilitates seeing what grace will be able to do later in their soul, if it corresponds with the due fidelity; because by attacking with all its strength only one of these fondnesses, he can triumph over it sooner, and the triumph of this victory foreshadows that of all the others.

The weakness of our nature is another reason that makes this practice highly recommended, not only to the principles of virtue, but also after moving forward over and over again on the path. *I can do everything in him who comforts me* [2], said the Apostle. But if human misery evades the efforts of grace more than once, and if the most discerning eye does not always see all the spots of our heart, it will not be authentic, and the truth of the Apostle being indisputable, that in a smaller circle we will be able to act with much greater strength, better distinguishing our faults, and applying the remedy more correctly and with happier success? The miserable man who so easily breaks the bravest and most generous purposes, will not be able to fulfill more exactly what he does to reform a part of the heart, than those who are directed to reform it in whole?

Lately, with this exercise the practice of virtue is smoothed to the soul. Our nature is so fond of variety that we have a kind of horror of a monotonous or uniform order of things. We always want to find new objects that catch our attention; the most pleasant things lose their attractiveness for us only by their continuation, and even the rest itself also exhausts us.

Grace usually by a thousand means sweetens the annoyance in souls that, for this reason, would generate in us a constant method of life. For a charm that is not given to man to explain, the faithful soul follows one year and another with pleasure practicing those same exercises of the previous years; and what for them would seem annoying and almost impossible to carry out, actually always seems pleasant to them, persevering in the same way all his life to achieve this happy dream.

Yet perhaps more than once there are among the ornaments of grace a natural inclination to dissipation that makes us long for new books, new advice, and even new directors, and they too in their new ministry. For the particular examination offers us the

---

[2] Phi 4,13

advantage of satisfying this appetite, and of giving an air of novelty to the practice of virtue.

While always keeping in mind the sight and scent of the beauty and fragrance of all the flowers of virtues, we hereby take them one by one to participate more closely in their benign influences, fall in love more firmly with its beauties, and ardently desire its benefits. Sometimes we put white purity before us, others the purple mortification, others the burning charity, and in this way we go through all the others successively, advancing at the same time in all; because the triumphs that we achieve over our appetites when we try to acquire only one, they prepare us to be victorious in the acquisition of the other virtues.

But what virtue should we choose preferably for the subject of our examination? And how long will we stop at one before moving on to the other? The answer to these questions will be brief, but the matter asks for some other explanations, which I am going to deal with after satisfying that one.

II. Content of the Particular Exam

Of course, those most urgent needs of the soul, that is, those more continuous and misguided defects to the neighbors with whom we live, demand a quicker remedy and for a long time enough to produce some improvement. I say some improvement, because if the bad inclination resists the efficacy of the remedy, it may well be possible to go to another virtue without always staying with it, since what has not been directly possible will be achieved little by little with the exercise of the other virtues: the prudence of a jealous director will know how to fix all this well.

More than knowing these needs so that they can manifest them to whom has to apply the remedy, or knowing how to apply it to oneself, is what we said to require here a detailed instruction on details quite curious and worthy of careful consideration.

When a soul detesting the unhappy state of mortal guilt, or that of a shameful inaction in which he has lived, begins to frequent the holy Sacraments, to give himself to prayer and other exercises of piety, it is said to enter the ways of virtue, or what is the same, that it is about perfection. But neither the Sacraments, nor prayer, nor other devout practices have the same perfection, but are the means by which grace communicates the supernatural forces, which wisely directed by the director, and their effects proven in the examinations, purify the heart of every stain, and consequently introduce virtue into it.

This doctrine is very interesting, as it explains the great usefulness of the devotional exercises and at the same time, their insufficiency for the achievement of the end that we seek; it silences the words of the foolish with whom they demonize piety, and discovers the deceit of those who, content with their practices, do not take care of the reform of the heart.

Purifying the heart is, therefore, the end of our frequency of the sacraments, of our supplications and of our examinations; purifying the heart not only of mortal sin, because even the most lazy and careless Christian must do it, but also of certain dispositions and attachments that are fruitful roots of a thousand resentments, anger, envy, displeasure, vain enjoyments, carelessness, omissions, and of I don't know what else.

This does not mean that the virtuous soul should never fall into any small fault. This would be impossible, according to the holy Council of Trent, without a special privilege that only the pure immaculate Mary had; all the other saints, says Saint Augustine, will be able to repeat the words of the beloved disciple: *If we said that we have no sin, we deceive ourselves, and we deceive also others* [3]. Keep this very much in mind the people of the world, who while being very lenient with their own, and who may also applaud their enormous crimes, are so finicky with

____

[3] 1 John 1: 8

others that at their slightest fault they are shocked, scandalized, and angry. They are full of zeal, but false zeal, since they demand more than the weak nature can. It is one thing to commit some small faults, and another to be fond of them; and it is not the same to ever betray out of human frailty the resolutions of grace, than to leave your evil inclinations alone without working to exterminate them.

I will also add that not every action that is supposed, and actually is contrary to virtue, deserves the name of sin, but only that of fault, defect or imperfection. Failure to follow this advice, not putting into practice the inspirations, failing the resolutions, not fleeing from certain occasions of sin and many others of the same kind, may be defects, whose neglect in amending them will deprive the soul of a thousand interior consolations; it will diminish the wealth of its merits, and will also prepare, although from afar, a fatal fall. But without breaking any law, precept or obligation, they can never be properly named sins.

From this belief comes an important warning, and it is that when a person who tries to achieve perfection falls into some venial sin, they deceive their confessor saying only that they have committed a fault against such virtue; because with this hypocritical language with which they want to cover up their frailty, they make the confessor believe that their fault has been similar to those in which human misery usually falls very frequently. And what will we say when with the same disguise one wants to confess certain or at least has the doubt of been serious sins? That such a confession is sacrilegious, for in it there have been hidden sins that should had been expressed.

Returning now to the matter from which the previous warnings diverted us, essential to be made by the trivial shyness of some people, and too much daring of others, I repeat, that perfection is achieved by purging the heart of vicious inclinations, and these are purged by introducing in it the virtues, which are nothing but habits that incline us to do good more easily.

There are many virtues that the soul practices for this, according to whether its good actions look at different objects, or offer a special difficulty in its execution. A simile will clarify well what I say. In the various needs that man experiences in human dealing, he does not have a single ability or strength to attend to all of them; And that is why there are many trades and jobs that are easily distinguished by anyone just knowing that one is destined to do one class of things, and the other is different. For likewise the soul cannot with a single good habit or virtue attend to all the obligations that it has with God, with its neighbors and with itself; It is necessary to multiply these habits according to the various kinds of actions with which it fulfills all the needs that derive from these three relationships, and each of them has its peculiar name, which makes known the functions to which it is destined, as love of God, obedience and so on.

However, since the soul is the same that has to carry out all its good actions by means of these virtues, and one also the end that is proposed with them, there is an intimate connection between the virtues that makes them go very united, helping the soul all together to achieve the triumph on its appetites, and increase grace and merit for eternal life.

In addition to that there is in our actions a particular thing, and it is that the same act can reflect various virtues or vices, depending on whether it is clothed with different circumstances. Anyone knows that the action of hurting a father is an offense done to a man, whom as such we have an obligation to love, and it is also an offense against a person to whom piety commands us to respect; for the same reason, defending him from such danger will be a doubly virtuous action, because it alone includes an act of charity towards the neighbor, and a present due to blood.

In virtues, as in all other things, it happens that one goes from the imperfect to the perfect. Virtuous actions are done that the beginnings with disgust, or at most with a passing ease, the effect of a certain sensible grace that lulls passions. The multiplied triumphs that over time the soul achieves on its appetites, and the repetition of acts later engenders in it a readiness, which results in causing joy and contentment in the practice of virtue; and thus overcoming almost all his vicious inclinations, there is in the soul a pure desire to seek God alone in all its works, a complete self-denial of itself, and a universal detachment not only of all things earthly, but also up to of heavenly favors and of all that does not lead to God.

III. How to make the particular exam

The particular exam must be done daily at noon and at night, or at least every night. This supposes the purpose of acquiring that virtue, or extinguishing that vice that is brought to examination, and the time to refresh the resolution is when getting up in the morning. For the people who make the prayer early in the morning, it suffices to make the resolutions that are taken there.

Three points contains this exercise. First: to ask God for grace to know the faults that have been committed on the proposed virtue. Second: to take notice of them, and write them down. Third: to be sorry and reaffirm the amendment if they have misbehaved, and while humbling themselves, attributing to God all their progress, and resolving to continue it with his help.

To put into practice the first point of asking God for the knowledge of our defects, those words of the Holy Job are very proper: *Tell me, Lord, how many iniquities and sins I have;*

show me my evils and my crimes [4]. Everyone can use these or similar words, as long as they come from the bottom of the heart, which is the main thing.

Like any action, this one either belongs to some virtue and it is at the same time contrary to some vice, or it belongs to some vice and is opposed to some virtue. There is between the virtues and their contrary vices a necessary connection that makes us know by faults the progress or failure, in the same way that happens with the light and the darkness that reject each other in such a way that as the darkness dissipates, the light also becomes more alive and effulgent. Being for this reason very important to know the number of our defects, it is advisable to write them down every day to compare them with those of the day or days before, and to know the result. For this purpose, three tables are placed at the end of this book[5], the first one designated to record the faults committed from one exam to the other; the second for the offenses committed from one confession to another, and the third for those of a whole month.

The person who believes he could know by only the number of the faults the strength of his passions and his advances in virtue would be very wrong. Their severity, duration, the most special graces to what they have resisted, and more abundant or stronger occasions that have occurred, are circumstances that cannot be reduced to calculation without a complication that is not within the reach of anyone, but which makes it very appropriate to take them into consideration. Who does not see the difference between two resentments, the one that passes quickly, and the other that continues for three or four hours, or a whole day? How much more robust does passion not manifest

---

[4] Cf. Job 13:23

[5] Ed note: the author assumes that the reader practices weekly confession.

itself in this second case, remaining firm against the efforts that grace will be making in all that time?

Finally, and the most important part of the particular examination, is the sorrow and resolution of the amendment. In vain will the soul inquire its iniquities and crimes, in vain will it make notes, in vain will it compare the faults of one day with those of the other; Alas! all this without sorrow and resolution is a mere pastime. Man can form plans and calculations to purify his heart; but it is not purified with accounts or merely human means. The tears of repentance in the falls, the confusion of our misery in the delays, and the humble recognition of the divine help in the progress made, are the only ones that can reform our hearts, and make fruitful our efforts in the examinations. We fall again and again, because satisfied with knowing what we have done or not done, we do not think of moving our hearts to the sorrow for our faults, nor the resolution of the amendment. We also fail after having succeeded and that is because we are proud of our progress and full of self-love, we do not take care into consideration with the humble confession that God alone is the author of this progress.

It is indispensable that we be persuaded intimately that the reform of the heart is the exclusive work of grace, and that without it all our efforts will end in failure. Grace, and only grace, is carving out in us the virtues, either sustaining us against the impetus of the passions and exciting us to feel sorrow for the falls, or by another means that I am now going to explain: the frequently repeated positive acts.

It happens at times that many of the virtues do not offer a person abundant opportunities to exercise them. In this case they can acquire virtue, advance greatly in it, and prepare their spirit very well to behave as it is appropriate to the occasions, imagining with vividness those circumstances in which they have fallen or could fall easily at other times, and moving his heart to desire to behave better again when that happens to them again: for example they refused to obey in something that was very repugnant to them. Well, bring this to mind many times, gathering in each one some reflection that encourages you to overcome that disgust, and it will be a means of acquiring the virtue of obedience.

But it is noteworthy that the nature of some virtues does not allow us to do this kind of practical acts by which we represent the occasions that we have had or may have, as happens with chastity, in which such memories would put us in a near danger that the occasions would turn into falls. In this case the acts can be reduced to a simple desire to possess that virtue, or to a repetition of the resolution that was made to acquire it. In any of the ways that are formed these acts that I call positive, produce a wonderful effect, repeated one or more times in each hour. For in addition to setting our hearts to conquer on those occasions, they are themselves true acts of virtue and meritorious before the eyes of God.

Since the use of these acts is so useful, it is especially convenient when the proposed virtue does not presents to us many occasions in which to exercise it, to set a certain number of them for the whole morning or all day, to examine their omissions, and list them separately from the faults, but with the same order in the tables that have the number series duplicated for this purpose. (See footnote 5)

I will now give knowledge of the virtues in particular. I will tell of the means of acquiring them, as I see fit, and of some of the various degrees to which they can be possessed. In several of them I divide the examination of sins and faults into two or more parts, which may very well serve separately as subject for this exercise. I do not express in the number of sins those that are serious, because I write for people who, if they ever seldom have the misfortune of falling into any of this kind, I suppose that they have enough instruction to distinguish the serious faults from the trivial in all the virtues, or what is the same, in the Commandments of the law of God and those of the Holy Mother Church, to which those are reduced.

Some may miss prudence and some other virtues; but having resolved to reduce their number as much as possible to accommodate myself to the capacity and circumstances of those who must make use of this booklet, rather than not to the scholastic rigor, I believe that some should be omitted because they are already taken for granted, like faith and hope. Others because I have grouped them in those that have some similarity among them, and others also because they are only for certain people in a very small number, such as clemency for the judges, and magnificence for the very opulent.

IV. About specific virtues

Love of God

This most noble virtue with which we love God well for his supreme goodness and infinite perfections, gives the luster to all the others, and receives subsistence from all of them; because love wants deeds. It establishes between God and us a real and true friendship, by virtue of which we look at his interests as our own, we are pleased with his excellences, we are glad that He is honored by his creatures, we feel the outrages that sinners do to him, and we wish to convert them all; and as love grows in us, the desire to remove the obstacles that prevent us from our union with him grows, and the horror of all faults, even of the slightest.

An effect of love is the continuous memory of the loved object, and in the love of God this continuous memory is also a very proper means to acquire the other virtues. For this reason, in examining the faults that can be committed against the love of God, the exercise of the divine presence will form the first part.

The means of acquiring this virtue are to frequently consider the many and invaluable benefits that we have received, especially from the Man God in the mysteries of his life, passion and death. Refer to the Creator all the beauties that we find in creatures, even those of those objects whose beauty tends to stir up the passions, intimately permeating themselves with the truth that all the charm of nature is nothing more than a droplet of the immense ocean of perfections that the Supreme Being contains; and directing the acts of all virtues to that which is the end of the law, and the substance of perfection: to obey for love, to be meek for love, to be humble, modest and chaste for love. Oh, and what an enhancement do the virtues practiced in this way receive! And what merits the soul accumulates for the day of the count!

From the desire to love God and to please Him in everything we do, results the purity of intention that makes us try in all things only His divine pleasure, whose exercise will form the third part of the following exam:

SINS AND FAULTS THAT MAY BE COMMITTED AGAINST THIS VIRTUE.

First Part.

1. To omit some of the times that they have resolved to remember God.

2. To not going to him for help in works of some importance.

Second part.

1. Not taking advantage of the inspirations with which God warns us to do good, and of the means to advance in virtue.

2. To expose themselves to any occasion to offend Him.

3. To not feeling pleased that God is honored by his creatures. 4. To show yourself indifferent when sinners offend him.

5. Not to take advantage of the opportunity to win a soul for Jesus Christ, or to extract some spiritual fruit.

6. To not caring to displease God, even slightly, or not doing his pleasure and will.

Third part.

1. To neglect to rectify the intention in everything we do.

2. To take ourselves as the main goal of our works, to show human respect, etc.

3. To mix into our actions vainglory or self-love.

Conformity with the will of God

The conformity with the divine will is a part of the love of God, that uniting the will of the lover to that of the beloved, makes him have the same will so as to want and not to want the same in all things, submitting to his dispositions equally in the prosperous as in the adverse. This is the great, the utmost, the substantial matter of love. And certainly that God has very indispensable titles to do everything that pleases him: all things are his, and he has done everything very well. For this reason, a soul in love with God would like to know in everything the will of the Lord, to act according to it always. And since in prosperity God conforms in a certain way to their will, they put the main care in overcoming his reluctance in adversity.

To know what pleases God, the following rules can be very useful: in things that do not depend on our will, let us be sure that as Job said: According to the Lord, this has been verified (cf Jb 1,21). In those that depend on us, if they are of obligation or of precept, the will of God is that we do them punctually; and if they are voluntary, the opinion of our superior, or in their absence that of any equal, is that of God, provided it is upright.

But note that in small works, as Saint Francis de Sales says, we must not pay attention to the annoying doubts with which the devil makes us lose the opportunity to practice many good works, while we are busy trying to discern which is the best. In deeds which do not make much difference from one to the other, why is this importune, and perhaps superstitious, care of wanting to know what God asks of us? In all things there may be excesses, which far from perfecting us in virtue, make us more imperfect. It is not a small conformity to submit oneself to act humbly without having this desired satisfaction that we please our divine Owner with that work; and this must be kept in mind more in the works of importance, when in spite of all the errands we see ourselves in the need of ever walking through darkness. It is these high dispositions of Providence, to which the creature must deeply humble his/her head.

SINS AND FAULTS THAT MAY BE COMMITTED AGAINST THIS VIRTUE.

1. Wanting madly that one thing happens rather than another.

2. Losing the tranquility, and even being inconsolable if it has not happened according to your desire.

3. Not lifting your heart to God in the setbacks of fortune, illness, death of relatives, temptations, dryness of spirit and other tribulations.

4. Not persuading yourself on these occasions that are all arranged for your good.

5. Showing some distrust in God in tribulations, or have angry thoughts against him.

6. To rejoice excessively when things come to us as we wanted.

7. Not taking care to find out what the will of God is, especially in things of importance.

Religion

After theological virtues there is no other more excellent than religion, which consists in giving God the honor and reverence He deserves. The greatness of God, the superiority of God, the sovereignty of God demand from us a respect and submission of spirit that must be manifested in the words, in the actions, and even in the posture of the body when we present ourselves before the throne of Divinity. Let us remember that if God, by his infinite goodness, deigns to admit us to his friendship, he does not stop being the great and powerful Lord, before whom the whole court in heaven bow deeply. Acts of this virtue are prayer and devotion; but as of the latter there is enough to say, I will form a separate matter from it, which will also include prayer in the examination of faults.

SINS AND FAULTS THAT MAY BE COMMITTED AGAINST THIS VIRTUE.

1. To affirm with oath something without enough need, even if it is true.

2. To listen with indifference to words injurious to the holy name of the Lord, or contrary to our faith and beliefs.

3. To speak of God and his saints with little respect.

4. To treat his images with irreverence.

5. To apply words from Holy Scripture to jokes, especially if they are not decent.

6. Not taking seriously what happens in the holy sacrament of Penance, Poking fun and taking as matter of fun the words that the confessor has said.

7. To make a vow lightly, exposing yourself not to fulfill it.

8. Breaking the resolutions with full consent.

9. To speak in the church unnecessarily, to laugh, to sleep or to be in a posture not as decent as the sanctity that place demands.

10. To not seek, within the possibilities, the proper decoration of the altars, the cleanliness and decorum of the Lord's house.

11. To disguise our religion in front of people for human respect, omitting the acts of reverence, genuflections and others that were customary.

12 To be ashamed of being seen as a devout person.

13. To prevent others from practicing their pious practices, without enough reason for doing so.

Devotion

People who make fervor and devotion consist of certain feelings noticeably overflowing our inferior are utterly mistaken. This is just an accidental effect of it that usually contributes to true devotion; but it also engenders in us a vain satisfaction, believing us much more advanced in the virtues than we really are. A will ready for everything that pleases God is what truly constitutes devotion, and this will may very well act promptly, and at the same time with disgust, annoyance, repugnance.

Saint Vincent de Paul never heard in the same position the second chime of the time he had determined to get up. See here a very prompt will that more than once would accompany the displeasure of the inferior. Our Savior was in the garden mired in mortal sadness, and yet how devoted was that prayer, *Father, not my will, but yours!*[6].

The means of acquiring devotion are: not burdening yourself with too many occupations, because these dissipate the spirit; not carrying out those that one has with calmness and tranquility without running over them, and not keeping one's soul in recollection, attracted as less as possible by external distractions.

SINS AND FAULTS THAT MAY BE COMMITTED AGAINST THIS VIRTUE.

1. Omitting prayer and exercises without cause

2. To shorten them for not liking them.

3. To not discard distractions promptly.

---

[6] Luke 22:42

4. To not follow to your best a schedule of hours for your exercises.

5. To shuffle the hours (of exercises) without necessity.

6. To not keep a method or not forming resolutions in prayer, nor to take any fruit from this and the other exercises.

7. To increase their devout practices to avoid work or because of another human motif.

8. To seek consolation in creatures in their afflictions.

9. To dispel your spirit with excessive recesses.

10. To be attached to sensitive feelings, falling into great sadness when deprived of them.

Charity with the neighbor

Charity with your neighbor is the same virtue as the love of God, who sees in all men a portrait of Him, a work of his hands. From this it follows that when we love someone who is a relative, or for having done us some favor, for their good manners, etc., we are not practicing the virtue of charity. We must be guided by a supernatural reason, because we love everyone without exception. We put up with the annoyances, the whims and the oddities of the people with whom we live; we should be helpful to all, solicitous to comfort them in their sorrows, careful to provide for their needs, attentive in advising them when it is convenient, exercise all the characteristics of the friendship even with strangers. These are the substantive works of a solid virtuous person who looks at the love of God and neighbor as the center of all his actions, as the fulfillment of all laws. And what a great thing it is to find even in the most remote and unknown countries so many faithful and attentive friends are animated by charity!

But where this virtue is known in a more unequivocal way, it is in the love of the enemies. Here there is no inclination of nature, nor human qualities, nor another motivation that regularly speaking, can move us. God alone, and only He is the author of this love.

Three attitudes or degrees should we climb up in this love of enemies. First: do not hate them; Second: wish them all well. Third: do good to them as much as possible.

SINS AND FAULTS THAT MAY BE COMMITTED AGAINST THIS VIRTUE.

1. Not to help the neighbor in some need, being able to.

2. Ridicule their words and actions.

3. To cause scandal so as to make them to offend God.

4. Treating them coldly, or not to want to talk to them for some period of time.

5. To avoid meeting or greeting them.

6. Make fun of them.

7. Not wanting to do what they like, while being able to do it without any inconvenience.

8. Not to suffer their impertinences and bad humor.

9. Telling to them jokes that we know they don't like.

10. Not to defend them when people speak ill of them.

11. To spread gossips among some people.

12. Not to give alms while being able to do it, or to give it reluctantly.

13. Being irksome on others, impertinent, annoying.

14. Speaking or hearing approvingly about others' faults, even if they are true and known to all.

15. Failure to correct their faults.

16. To give them some bad advice or not to give them good advice when they need it.

17. To not console them when they are sad.

18. To praise them without sufficient reason, moving them to vainglory.

19. Having idle and useless conversations with them.

20. To despise them internally.

21. To love them for human reasons, and not for God's sake.

22. To show resentment, coldness or rancor to them.

23. To feel sorry that they are esteemed and well regarded, and to be glad when they are despised or forgotten.

Justice

This is a virtue with which we give each one his due. The matter of this virtue is very vast, since it includes the entire fifth, seventh and tenth commandments of the Decalogue, and part of the sixth, eighth and ninth according to whether we harm others physically, or the fidelity in marriage, or don't respect their honor, or their fame or their assets. And although virtuous people hardly commit such injustices in an overt way, nevertheless, own interest and greed often precipitate them more than once to harming others in trifles, or in things where injustice is not immediately obvious.

The means of acquiring this virtue is to always side with others, thinking, speaking and doing for them the same as we would like them to think, speak and do for us. Good means for not harming others in their property are also detaching the heart of love for riches, and not deciding by our own judgment in doubtful cases in favor of our own interests, because we are always very bad judges of ourselves.

I classify the examination of this virtue into two parts; In the first, I put everything pertaining to the damage that can be done to the neighbors in their property; in the second, the injustices that damage their honor and fame. On the other aspects, there is no much to say in an examination of minor offenses.

SINS AND FAULTS THAT MAY BE COMMITTED AGAINST THIS VIRTUE.

First Part.

1. Wasting some of the materials they have given us in order to make a dress or any other useful object.

2. To keep the remainders from the cloth that they have given you.

3. For the servants, do not save what they can prudently in what they buy for the house and in what they spend on it.

4. To spend on their own errands the time for which they are paid their wages or salary.

5. For employers to demand to work longer without paying for the overtime.

6. To not allow enough food for the employees to eat.

7. Be very petty towards those who serve and work, not giving their works the value and payment they deserve.

8. Delaying the payment of bills or debts.

9. Make use of other people's things more than that granted by their owner.

10. To bargain excessively, forcing the seller to sell for a very low price.

11. The seller exaggerates the good qualities of the things, that they deceive the buyer and make them pay more than it is worth.

12. To not return the small amounts that you have mistakenly been given in an account, or to want to pay with false currency.

13. Take advantage of the need of others to buy or sell at an unfair price, or to lend money with usury.

14. Not doing enough errands to find the owner of the lost and found thing.

15. To desire other people's jewelry, dresses, etc.

Second Part.

1. To say of the neighbor some fault that they have not committed.

2. To say those faults that are true, but hidden, without sufficient reason for it.

3. To embarrass them by revealing their faults, or showing them in their face.

4. To read their private papers, their letters and other secrets that they did not want us to know.

5. Interpret their indifferent or perhaps good actions as bad.

6. Blame them on something they haven't done.

7. Judge or suspect them without a good reason.

Piety

Among our neighbors there are some with whom the bonds of flesh and blood compel us to exercise more especially acts of charity and justice. The virtue with which we practice these duties is called piety, which requires of us first with parents and then with other relatives according to the degrees of kinship. Since virtue does not want gingerbreads when it comes to fulfilling the great and sublime commandment of charity, it sometimes asks us to delay and even omit entirely our devotions to help our neighbor; but this which is demanded from us even to any stranger, demands much more to those of our own. So a son or daughter who needing their parents consolation to ease their sorrows, remained withdrawn in their room and did not adapt themselves with the circumstances, seeking relief with an honest recreation, would have a virtue of convenience that does not know how to leave God for God, when he himself wants it.

But also a too carnal love often produces the servile fear of upsetting parents at times and in things that are clearly known to be harmful to their soul; and in that case it would be better to leave them unhappy than to satisfy worldly and perhaps irreligious desires. This excessive love for relatives is not as harmful to anyone as to people who have already died to the world and who live only for God in religion. Why should a nun turn her eyes to those objects from which she generously shed herself forever? If you want to have peace with yourselves in religion, let the dead bury their dead.

SINS AND FAULTS THAT MAY BE COMMITTED AGAINST THIS VIRTUE.

1. To deal with parents and relatives in a bad mood, hard and harsh.

2. Do not console them when they are sad, nor take an interest in their things.

3. To have more attention to strangers than to yours.

4. To easily condescend with parents to attend dangerous meetings.

5. For parents, to love a son more than another, using with the first of preferences that excite jealousy to the second one.

Obedience

This important virtue that makes ready the will to execute the advice or orders of the legitimate superior is part of the observance that gives parents and elders the honor and respect they deserve.

Obedience has three degrees, which I will consider in the examination of faults. First grade: to obey promptly. Second: to conform one's will with that of the superior, *to want the same thing, and to reject the same thing*[7]. Third: also shape your judgment, firmly persuading yourself that things are very well ordered.

To overcome the difficulty that nature has to subject itself to another, the following two considerations will be very useful. The first is that with obedience we offer God the greatest sacrifice we can, the sacrifice of our will, which is the most excellent and dear thing we have.

The second, that the superior, be it father, husband, master or any other authority, acts in the place of God unless they command something manifestly evil. And consequently we cannot err in obeying them, even if they err in what they command us, because their will is that of God.

These two reasons, with which obedience is so kind to anyone who wants to be saved, make it much more so for those who seek perfection. This is a shortcut to heaven, a sure path in which all steps taken, that is, all works are carried out, bear the seal of God's approval. Blessed is the soul that leaves itself entirely in the hands of the one who acts on earth on behalf of

---

[7] For the Romans *"idem velle, idem nolle"* [same desires, same dislikes] was a definition of friendship.

God, and who is resolved to do nothing by their own will, but by that of their spiritual guide! What comfort will they have in setbacks when they remember that it was not their whim that moved them into disgrace, but an order from heaven communicated by their director!

But this entire docility to obey the spiritual director, also requires a great frankness to reveal the bottom of the heart with all the clarity that allows the gravity of the holy court, and the nobility of dealing with a man. Few documents are more important than this in the life of the spirit: *Unless you become like children, you would not enter the kingdom of heaven*[8]. Children in simplicity and submission; children to say everything without duplicity and to obey without meddling to examine the superior's commands; but children after having been successful in choosing the one who is to rule your souls.

SINS AND FAULTS THAT MAY BE COMMITTED AGAINST THIS VIRTUE.

First Part.

1. Not doing the thing that were ordered to do or fulfilling a duty.

2.To do it, but to do it later, only after finishing what one was doing.

3. To do something without asking for a permit, for which you presumed that it would not be granted.

4. To do something wrongly for taking revenge on the superior.

---

[8] Mt 18, 3

5. Search for excuses so that the director is satisfied and does not force them to do what he has ordered.

6. To hide their true feelings or dispositions to the director.

Second Part.

1. To obey reluctantly without putting our heart into it.

2. To imply in the way we behave that one obeys reluctantly.

3. Being more ready or having a greater liking to obey some things more than others.

4. Use of certain schemes so that they don't command you to do what you don't like

5. Not taking care of pleasing the superior when they manifest their will without expressly commanding you out of consideration.

6. Not to consider that the superior represents the very person of God who commands.

Third part.

1. Contradict the superior or reply to them with bad humor.

2. Criticize or murmur that this was not well ordered.

3. To persuade yourself that the superior errs in what they command.

4. To ask them for an explanation as to why they order that.

5. Not saying it but having inner desire that they give us this explanation.

6. Discuss whether what they ordered was the right thing or not.

Affability

Piety, which, as Saint Paul says, *is useful for everything*[9], also gives devout people rules of a fine education; rules that if not adapted to the whim of men and their latest fashions, have the advantage of being adaptable to all countries and at all times. In fact, affability, or friendship as Saint Thomas also calls it, is that virtue that moderates our actions and words, so that we are pleased with others in human dealing, which is perfectly appropriate to courtesy in opinion of an illustrious writer of the last century.

A person who possesses this virtue speaks to their elders with respect, to their equals with decorum, to their inferiors without haughtiness, and to all in a way that makes our company appealing. This person is grateful for favors, attentive without flattering, surrendered without baseness, and a friend of keeping with all the consideration they deserve. Tis person uses compliments, ceremonies and offers that are, not the cold expression of lips that do not agree with the heart, but the effect of a burning charity, which wants to do good to all, without upsetting any.

They are also restrained in their words, letting others speak in turn; they always run away from the lie, but the truth is bitter, either hide it or say it sweetened in a way that makes it less hard to those who have to hear it. They use some white jokes in his conversations, never using those that may be offensive, unseemly or unpleasant. They are attentive to visit those that the obligation or their class requests; but avoid being annoying, making many visits or very long, or in times that are not appropriate.

---

[9] 1Timothy, 8

They also extend their care and charity to the sick; but to these only speak what, how, when and as to their state of indisposition is convenient. In short, try everything that pleases, and avoid everything that displeases others. These are the rules to be observed in the sweet virtue of affability. Among them I have included not telling lies, because these are profane, and very unpleasant to those who hear them; but as the lie belongs to the virtue of truthfulness, I form a separate part of it in the following examination.

SINS AND FAULTS THAT MAY BE COMMITTED AGAINST THIS VIRTUE. TRUTHFULNESS.

1. To tell lies for hobby.

2. Say them to avoid any quarrel or rebuke.

3. To use in their words duplicity foreign to the Christian simplicity.

4. To tell lies that can put some people at odds, or cause some other light damage.

SINS AND FAULTS THAT MAY BE COMMITTED AGAINST THIS VIRTUE. AFFABILITY.

1. Not corresponding to the benefit received, nor giving due thanks for it.

2. To talk too much in the conversation.

3. To interrupt the one who is speaking.

4. To argue or quarrel with another.

5. Giving to somebody unpleasant news without need, or not using a few detours that prevent their spirit from hearing it calmly.

6. To be too serious in dealing with people.

7. To use jokes that are unworthy of their character, or annoying to those around them.

8. To pretend ostentation or much knowledge

9. To give yourself a tone of superiority or of teacher to others.

10. To be inopportune in the visits.

11. To disturb the sick by speaking to them what they do not like, or with a strong voice, in times or more than what is convenient for them.

12. Do not give up the position or the sidewalk when and to whom it is due.

13. At the table do not seek all possible cleanliness and tidy up.

14. Cause nausea or annoyance with some action or word.

Mortification

The first request that Jesus Christ makes to the one who wants to be his disciple, is to deny themselves. This is the reason why, after having spoken about the virtues towards God and towards our neighbor, when going to deal with those that look towards ourselves I have given first place to mortification, which in part is the same as denial of one's will.

This virtue holds the flesh to the spirit and releases it from certain inclinations that prevent it from believing in good, and helping to fly to the height of perfection. Accordingly, mortification can be either exterior or interior; that is subjected to the spirit or to the body. Following this division, the examination of the faults will have two parts: The first is about the five senses of the body, and the second about the three powers of the soul.

The world looks at devout people as strong willed people, friends of convenience who always get their way; and it must be admitted that this perception is not entirely unfounded; but if you work to acquire this virtue, you will solemnly deny with your works those ill-will sayings. But everything requires moderation and prudence and if these are not observed in a virtue in which all our actions, even the good ones or the indifferent ones, can give us the opportunity to exercise it, it is very easy for a person who is too thoughtful, or who wants to advance a lot in a short time, to give to an extreme that take away from your freedom of spirit, and also ruin your health. The body needs its breaks, and the soul its outlets and entertainments that somehow recreate it, which is also a virtue, a virtue that the Greeks call *eutropelia*.[10]

SINS AND FAULTS THAT MAY BE COMMITTED AGAINST THIS VIRTUE.

First part.

1. To leave undone the usual mortifications without a just reason.

2. Not to ask the director for mortifications that their health allows them, or to do them without his license.

3. To be very delicate in suffering the cold, the heat, the pains of illnesses and other inconveniences.

4. To seek the delight and comfort of the body.

5. To complain about the uncomfortable bed or about anything else that has given you an opportunity to suffer.

6. To speak useless words.

7. To not ever mortify yourself in not watching something you wanted; the ear in not hearing pleasant conversations and music; and smell when a bad smell is perceived.

8. Being lazy to get up, to work intensely and to other similar demanding tasks.

9. Wasting time on useless visits and conversations.

Second part.

---

[10] N of E. Eutropelia: Virtue that moderates the excess of amusements or entertainments; Innocent speech, game or occupation, which is taken by way of honest recreation with temperance.

1. To not reject useless thoughts.

2. To remember on purpose the events that are pleasant in your memory.

3. To ask and know what is not your business.

4. On the contrary, being careless in learning the necessary or useful things for your soul and for the fulfillment of your obligations.

5. Not to suffer the harshness of the bad tempered, or rustic people and other annoyances that our neighbors give us.

6. The superiors do not suffer the defects of their servants and their voluntary negligence.

7. The inferiors do not suffer the arrogance with which they are ordered, the lack of consideration with which they demand excessive work from them, or the fact that they are given more tasks than others.

8. To not forget the injury received.

9° To be attached to money.

10. Not to accommodate as much as possible to the taste of others in the choice of a stroll, in the entertainment class, and in a thousand other things that are usually offered.

11. Not to overcome certain aversions or dislikes that naturally we have towards some people.

12. To not let go of your heart from the attachment to the things of your use, and from everything that attracts you with excess.

13. Not to mortify also the taste that we feel in some things that we necessarily have to do, like eating.

Patience

Patience should not be confused with meekness; this serves to contain the bursts of anger, and that to suppress the sadness of present evils, the despondency or lack of spirit that results from being sick, or having any other setbacks. This suffering must have as its object not only the evils themselves, but also their consequences. Namely we are sick; then not only do we have to suffer with resignation and with pleasure the disease, but also not being able to work, spending on medicines, being annoying to those who have to take care of us, etc. We must suffer without complaining or referring to them, because self-love regularly always exaggerates our pains or discomforts. In addition to that we bother others with similar complains, even if it seems to us that they listen to us with great interest.

This virtue has three degrees. First: do not show sadness to others. Second: to repress it internally. Third: desiring and enjoying difficulties.

The means to acquire this virtue are: consider the works of Jesus Christ, the prize that is reserved for the person who is patient, the uselessness of not wearing sufferings with pleasure, and that they are a clear signal of the love and affection of our good God.

SINS AND FAULTS THAT MAY BE COMMITTED AGAINST THIS VIRTUE.

1. To complain that God abandons you.

2. To ponder their sufferings over and over again, and to want everyone to express their pity and take part in their sorrows.

3. To be continuously talking about those pains to everyone.

4. To deject yourself so that you do not want to receive comfort from anyone.

5. Be heartbroken or be in a bad mood because of difficulties.

6. Judging that God sends you too many contradictions.

7. To waste yourself internally because of the setbacks.

Meekness

I have already said that meekness restrains the movements of anger, and everyone knows that this is an appetite for revenge. Self-love often makes us commonly believe that our anger and upsets are always very fair, that the temperament of such a person, that the coincidence of such an event in certain circumstances were enough reasons to ignite the wrath of the most holy of the men. But let us keep in mind that a soft heart never breaks, and that if we had a good amount of sweetness, we would not be so easily bothered, and would not cause such a great fuss of the people who treat us.

We must not only exercise meekness with our neighbors, but also with ourselves. Some people seeing how easily they fail and break their resolutions, are exasperated and can hardly suffer themselves; but far from reprimanding themselves harshly they should be encouraged to rise from their falls with new breath, having sympathy for their own misery.

The means of acquiring meekness are: remembering that it was the favorite virtue of Jesus Christ, the one that attracted the gentiles of the first centuries to Christianity, and the one that today conquers the hearts of the neighbors with whom we live.

SINS AND FAULTS THAT MAY BE COMMITTED AGAINST THIS VIRTUE.

1. To reprimand without just cause for our bad mood.

2. To do it with reason, but with untempered voices.

3. To throw objects with anger or fury, shouts or kicks,

4. To look down on somebody, or to show to them with deeds or words the anger that we have towards them.

5. Be upset against animals, or against anything that has done us any harm, delayed our work, etc.

6. Not wanting to eat or do other things, for being angry.

7. Showing movements of restlessness or anger.

8. Desire to take revenge or to do something to show resentment for any injury committed towards us.

Humility

If the love of God gives splendor to the other virtues, humility serves as a foundation that keeps them firm, and without it they will not be able to survive long. This virtue, which consists of a habit that restrains the desires to overcome and surpass the others is extremely necessary for us, because pride was the sin of the first man; pride is our first inheritance from corrupted nature; pride is the one that transpires in most of our actions and the one that unfortunately steals a great part of our merit. The illusions that we form here are very worthy of pity. It seems to us that we attract a lot of people's attention, that we are highly esteemed or that our works are very thorough and accomplished; and hence the sorrow, the feeling, and the deep sadness that we have when the behavior that others observe with us makes us know that we were deceived.

In many ways and to many degrees they tend to study this virtue; But I will distinguish three types of humilities, which will form as many aspects in the examination of faults: humility of knowledge, humility of affection and external humility.

The knowledge of our nothingness is the root of all humility; but knowledge not vague and speculative but practical that firmly convinces us that what we have of good and excellent is on loan; that sin alone is ours, and that even when we receive from God the greatest favors and serve as admiration to the whole world, we know how to distinguish well between what is ours and what is not, without attributing any of this to ourselves. This seems very easy and is nevertheless in practice the most arduous and sublime.

This knowledge and persuasion of our misery will make us glad when others form the same concept of us and this is the humility of affection. Hence the contempt for praise, the lack of care to be pleased, to appear good, and to attract the attention of others, and the joy and happiness of their sayings, their ridicule and denigration towards us.

From this love for abjections, the desire is born to put our sight and that of others in our nothingness, in furniture, in clothing, companies, occupations, words and so on, which is external humility. But be careful since self-love is very subtle, and is introduced through the cracks of these external things. We speak badly about our works, and we attribute defects to them so that others may ponder them; and we gladly say that we are sinners or lukewarm, so that they call us just and fervent, using the same humility to feed our pride.

The means of achieving this virtue are: the example of Jesus Christ our Lord; considering the vileness of the opposite vice, because no arrogant person wants to be known. Instead they put the means to be esteemed; the great peace that the contempt of those points of honor, of those snubs and sayings that so much unpleasantness usually cause to the proud, puts to our soul; and lately, the exercise of external humility.

SINS AND FAULTS THAT MAY BE COMMITTED AGAINST THIS VIRTUE.

First part.

1. To form of oneself and their abilities a judgment superior to what really is.

2. To persuade oneself that what they do or say is better done or said than that of the others.

3. To believe that one occupies an important place in the world, and that great attention should be paid to him.

4. To have satisfaction that your opinion is followed.

5. To always want to get away with it.

6. To dispute without reason; and when there is reason, to do it with stubbornness or in a bad way.

7. To give your opinion without being asked, unless it is demanded by charity.

8. To despise the opinion of others.

9. Do not looking at all your gifts and abilities as borrowed.

10. Not believing yourself unworthy of all honor and esteem, and even of the land that you tread on and all the things that you possess.

Second part.

1. To put means to be appreciated.

2. To cite yourself as example in conversations.

3. To pretend more than one is, either in virtue, or in temporal things.

4. Excusing oneself when rebuked.

5. Cover up the director some humiliating faults, so as not to lose the good concept which he has of them.

6. To listen with pleasure to the praises they give them, or to be glad that they have spoken well of them,

7. Desires to please.

8. To be sad for suffering some humiliation or contempt.

9. To be sad for the fact that others are more esteemed, or play a more important role in the world.

10. To savor on purpose in thoughts of things that honor us.

Third part.

1. To refuse to do menial tasks.

2. Postures and gestures of vanity.

3. To seek for or desire to be singled out.

4. Words in their own praise or that imply their virtue, their abilities, the illustriousness of their family, etc.

5. Words in self contempt, so that they form good judgment or tell you otherwise.

6. To have disgust of been accompanied with people of lower class.

7. To be ashamed of poor dress, of the few pieces of furniture and the like.

Chastity

The merit of chastity must be great when, even in the world itself, it is regarded as an affront to let oneself be carried away by the desires of impurity that this virtue tries to restrain. Uncommon garment, and how much it ennobles the human species! To live with the flesh and act according to the spirit, be a man and behave like an angel. Garment admirable that makes the virgin wives of the Lamb, who will place in their hands a very leafy palm, and on their heads a double crown!

But also if this beautiful virtue comes from heaven, it lives very exposed in the treatment of the earth. Such a delicate flower thrives only among the thorns of mortification and the flight of occasions; and in no other is it more necessary than in this to pay attention to small things, and to be prompt and generous to reject temptations. Because the person who in this despises the little, or is lazy in shaking importunate thoughts, is close and very close to a great fall. An excessive affability with people of the other sex, the tender and loving words, the platitudes and the too familiar treatment, are sparks that if they are not extinguished quickly, they burn the whole soul. The infatuations, these foolish loves to which young people tend to have such a fondness, are networks stretched out at their feet to entangle them in a thousand guilts, after making them slaves of a vile passion.

Shame also preserves purity, which the Lord's goodness gave to the sinner at the very moment when by his disobedience he became a slave to his passions; and it was a particular providence that, in the weaker sex, it would be the largest, in order to better guard herself against the assaults of the strongest. How good the blushing face of a young woman seems, a sign of her modesty, when she talks to any man!

Do not believe those who are not young people exempt from practicing this virtue: here there is no exemption for even one. Even the freedom of marriage has its chaste limits, outside of which it ceases to be a holy state.

SINS AND FAULTS THAT MAY BE COMMITTED AGAINST THIS VIRTUE.

1. Do not keep much decency with yourself in all your actions.

2. Touching another person or letting themselves be touched in the hands, head, face, etc.

3. Look at someone when they get naked or get dressed.

4. To read some book or magazine about romantic love.

5. Look at dangerous paintings.

6. To keep looking to a person of the other sex.

7. To sing a sensual song.

8. To listen to dangerous conversations or songs.

9. To speak alone for a long time or very often with a person of the opposite sex without just cause.

10. To receive or make a gift to someone of the other sex who has to whom we feel an inclination.

11. To be very eager to be with a person whenever possible, without ever succeeding in separating from them or getting tired of talking to them.

12. In the absence of this person to defend them with fervor and be glad that they speak well of such a person.

13. Have some jokes or straightforwardness with them.

14. Give rise to temptations due to lack of caution.

15. Be lazy or careless in discarding them promptly when they come.

16. To think or speak about something that is lawful for you, but that can awaken evil thoughts.

Temperance

It is more difficult, according to some, to enjoy a delight with measure, than to deprive oneself entirely, and this is what happens to us with food. It is necessary to eat, and God has made the act with which we satisfy this need. But our flawed nature has turned a means of conservation into the end of our desires, looking for food only for taste and even to the extreme of sometimes destroying with excesses our health that was supposed to preserve.

The faults list that is put on the exam will reveal all the rules of temperance; rules that, although difficult to always observe exactly, are nevertheless very important in the Christian life; because intemperance obscures our understanding, disables it for prayer, causes vain joys, loquacity, immodesty, lustful gestures and impurity.

Fasting is a means of acquiring temperance. But more constant, and therefore more effective, is a continuous moderation that makes us always get up from the table with the desire of eating a bit more.

SINS AND FAULTS THAT MAY BE COMMITTED AGAINST THIS VIRTUE.

1. To eat food in excess.

2. To drink too much wine.

3. Eating intensely and eagerly, seeking more delight than just repairing the need of food.

4. To eat in a hurry or with anxiety.

5. To look for very tasty delicacies in our food.

6. To want our meals to be seasoned always to our preferred taste.

7. To eat something when you feel like it without waiting for the appointed time.

8. To complain when the food is not well served.

9. Not depriving oneself from eating something that you know will not be healthy for you.

10. To be continuously talking about food.

11. To spare too much time yourself thinking about what you are going to eat or have already eaten.

Modesty

That interior reflexion with which a virtuous soul lives, is shown in their prayer to God but also when they are alone, and in their speech with people. They maintain a certain calm serenity in their spirit that communicates to all their external appearance; and this is what we call modesty. Their body movements, their spoken words and in the clothing and adornment, edify the neighbors with whom they live, because it is like glimpsing the perfection that is hidden inside.

This external appearance is important also in young people. It preserves their purity when used well. The most daring man is restrained by a modest exterior, and this mirror in which he sees portrayed the candor of innocence produces such an effect, that perhaps he comes to venerate as an angel whom he was going to offend as a woman.

But it is necessary that the actions come out with the naturalness that interior modesty gives them; otherwise it is a mere hypocrisy that annoys and bothers others, especially when things are taken to an extreme that clearly reveals the affectation.

SINS AND FAULTS THAT MAY BE COMMITTED AGAINST THIS VIRTUE.

1. To walk with too much precipitation.

2. To move the arms and head continuously

3. Be seated in a position that can move thus to laughter or excite the imagination of others in a wrong way.

4. To take little precaution in covering the arms, breasts and other parts with the greatest decency possible.

5. To speak loudly without need and in a haughty voice.

6. To laugh in a disproportionate way.

7. To take part in all the conversations, and meddle in what is not our business.

8. To bring our eyes continuously from place to place, watching everything that happens.

9. To use jokes and pranks with people at times that require a serious environment.

10. Wearing clothes that attract a lot of attention due to their color or shape, especially when we are going to receive the Holy Sacraments.

11. Decorate and compose more than what your class allows and what your state and circumstances demand.

12. To walk in a disheveled, torn or filthy dress.

Conclusion

Among the virtues that I have just explained, and whose beautiful qualities you will have fallen in love with, and also aroused the desire to put into practice the means that I have pointed out to acquire them, one is missing. This virtue will crown your efforts, and without it all the others will be useless. And this one is PERSEVERANCE.

When the devil, furious by the spiritual growth that with the exercise of the virtues you will have treasured, wants to wreck the ship of your soul in the stumbling block of inconstancy. When your friends with their foolish talk try to separate you from the practice of good, or when an annoying boredom follows you everywhere puts you in danger of returning from the beginning or the middle or perhaps very near the end of your career, stick with perseverance. Shake with it the annoying thoughts and disgust that the tempter brings you. Revive your spirit. Gather new strength to acquire with the help of private examination all the virtues, and continue constant in your exercise, until death, which removes from the worldly one their momentary and petty happiness. Dead leads you to what is permanent and plentiful, where the God to whom you have been faithful in time will be your reward in eternity.

❦

Appendix First

A dialogue for the instruction of doing the Spiritual Exercises

Q. What do spiritual exercises come to be?

A. Although this name can be given, and is given to any exercise ordered for the good of the soul, such as meditating, praying, examining the conscience, etc., spiritual exercises are more properly called a series of days used especially in the seek of salvation.

Q. Who was its author?

A. Strictly speaking, the divine Master himself taught us by example, when he began his preaching for forty days in the desert; and he also commanded his disciples to do so, when He returned from the mission, he said to them: "*Come now to rest*"[11] and He led them to solitude. But the exercises in the form that are practiced now, are due to Saint Ignatius of Loyola, who composed them while in the cave of Manresa doing penance shortly after his conversion. And even though he was a rude man without a formal education, they have produced copious fruits, and the Supreme Pontiffs have filled them with praise, looking at them as a work divinely inspired for the good of souls.

Q. For whom are they convenient?

R. To everyone: to the righteous and sinners, these who desire to change their lives, and those who want to make new advances in virtue, or to revive their fervor if it began to decline. But since many and very excellent books have been written to help sinners

---

[11] *Mk 6, 31*

in this holy undertaking, and on the other hand, the little book in which this instruction is inserted, will only be handled by devout people, everything I am going to say here will be written only for the spiritual good of these souls; because although the exercises are for everyone, the way of doing them varies according to the end that each one sets out, and the particular dispositions in which one finds oneself.

Q. Are the exercises very effective to achieve the goal of converting, or perfecting, etc., that the person intends?

R. So much so that if, after having done them, the exerciser does not feel any good effect on his soul, he can already assure himself without fear of being wrong, that he has not been faithful in observing the rules that have been prescribed, or that he took this exercises with much indifference.

Q. Where does the great effectiveness of the exercises come from?

A. From three things that are highly recommended. Each of them appear in the holy Scriptures, and they are explained here as follows.

Q. What are they?

A. Meditation on eternal truths; the quality of the truths that are mainly meditated in the exercises, and the way in which they are meditated. Of the meditation says Jeremías [12], that the cause of seeing the earth in such extreme desolation, is that no one meditates these truths in their hearts.

Of the quality of the truths that are meditated on in the exercises, and which are mainly the *Novissimis*[13], the book of

---

[12] Desolatione desolata est omnis terra, quia nullus est qui recogitet corde. Jerem., c. XII. v. 11

[13] Ed Note: The Last Things: Death, Last Judgement, Hell, Glory

Ecclesiastes says[14] they are the remedy for never sinning. Lately, the way of meditating, which is separated from the bustle of creatures, is the same that the Lord requires for Hosea to speak to the soul, to the heart.

Q. According to this, the exercises do not consist in praying all day, nor in attending some practices that are held in the temple for a few moments or hours?

A. No; that's a huge mistake; and those who do not do anything else, do not expect to obtain the copious fruits that are promised to those who do the holy exercises.

Q. Well, how are they to be done?

R. Meditating a lot, and with much attention, those very important truths of our religion, separated as much as possible from all the businesses or objects that can take this attention away from us.

Q, To better understand this I would like to know how many and what are the things that make up the whole of the spiritual exercises?

R. Six things. First and very necessary is the retreat; second, the mental prayer; third, the spiritual reading; fourth, the examinations of conscience; fifth, the internal and external mortification, and sixth, the vocal prayer. I will talk about each one of them in particular.

---

[14] In omnibus operibus tuis memorare novissima tua, et in aeternum non peccabis. Eccle. c. VII. v. 40.

Recollection

This is at the heart of the exercises, and without it nothing or very little will help to do well mental prayer, which is like the substance of them. Every day we are seeing that when a man has to deal with another a matter of great interest, he calls him aside, and takes him to a place where no one can interrupt them. And if it happens that they talk where there is people in the vicinity, or children shouting, or noise of any kind, then they say to each other "Here we are not in the proper place to deal with this matter." Well, in this way, to deal with the most serious thing that man has, which is his salvation, the best would be to materially withdraw to a solitary place; but since few will have the opportunity to do so, at least efforts must be made to seek solitude in the middle of the world in the best possible way.

For this purpose, the one practicing the spiritual exercises must abstain from all distractions and avoid unnecessary visits. They must also be able to get rid of all business and temporary occupations as much as they can, which are not required by their position or obligation. They should be able to freely dispose of time, and not to be distracted by occupations, even if they are in themselves lawful and good. And in addition to getting rid of every distraction entirely, they must try to remove from the imagination and memory all thoughts that may disturb them in their meditations, keeping their heart calm and free of any human affection.

Saint Ignatius considered this recollection as important, that in order for the exerciser to achieve it, he did not hesitate to descend to such detailed rules as those that we are going to say, and that nobody should despise them trying to do the exercises with perfection. *"Not wanting to think of joyous things, such as glory, etc., to be sorrowful and recognize their sins more clearly,"* is the 6th note or addition that the saint puts for the first days of exercises, to which the 7th also belongs to: *"deprive yourself of all clarity, closing the windows, except for reading and eating"*; the 8th is *"not to laugh or say something that provokes laughter"*; and the 9th is *"to restrain the eyes and curiosity, unless he has to receive or dismiss someone."*

Mental prayer

If the recollection is so necessary for the soul to hear the voice of God, the time when we must mainly hear this voice it is that of mental prayer.

Four times can be used for it and one hour in each time. Times are in the morning, around noon, in the afternoon and at night. San Ignacio sets a fifth time at midnight; but this is generally omitted, and even that of the afternoon can be reduced to half an hour or three-quarters, because it is the time when nature is least ready for mental operations. The matters to be meditated upon at least the first days are: the last things (end of man, sin, death, judgment and hell); but speaking to devout people, it will be better that after occupying the first days of these truths that one moved by fear, meditate on others that move by a more noble principle. Such are: the Incarnation of the Son of God, the internal and external pains of Jesus in his most holy passion, and God's love for men.

To do the mental prayer well, Saint Ignatius instructs that one or two steps before arriving to the place we are going to pray, we stop for the time of an Our Father and think that God is looking at us, immediately doing an act of humility. It is understood that that's when the prayer is not held in public. With regard to what is to be done in the morning, he also instructs for the night before to think about the point to be meditated while trying to fall asleep, and in awakening by remembering it again, representing oneself while dressing, some images similar to what he is going to meditate. For example, if it is in mortal sin, then imaging oneself ugly and disgusting; in judgment as a prisoner, etc.

In addition, it must be kept in mind that on the days of exercise, the plan for amending one's sins and defects, it is better to do so outside this time. It must not be brought to prayer, but rather one must have a general desire to improve life, and to take advantage of the means that are more fit, as the Lord himself inspires those who speak more closely to the soul in these precious days.

After the prayer is over, a quarter of an hour will be spent thinking about how you have been doing, which can be done sitting or walking. If you find that the prayer went wrong you will see what the cause has been for it and you will be sorrow for it. And if it went well, thank God, and try to do it the same way again.

Spiritual Reading

This can be considered as a kind of mental prayer and therefore is very important, particularly to those who are not well versed in meditating, which will sometimes get more fruit from reading if they do it well. Four other times alternate with the prayer times are to be used, but half an hour of reading will suffice each time. The materials for this reading can be taken from the book of *Kempis*[15], from the *Spiritual Combat*[16], *Exercises of Father Rodríguez*[17], *Practice of love for Jesus Christ*[18] and others. You could also have a reading every day in the life of a saint or saints more suited to your circumstances, and another in some instruction for the practical exam.

As the purpose of these readings is not precisely to know what the book says. but to be familiar with its content, it is necessary that the spiritual reading is done with pause, stopping at what moves you the most, without striving to read as much, but to entertain that half an hour with profit and good sentiments, for which the Holy Spirit must be invoked before asking for his help.

---

[15] *The Imitation of Christ* is a Christian devotional book by Thomas à Kempis, first composed in Latin (as *De Imitatione Christi*) ca. 1418–1427

[16] The Spiritual Combat, Lorenzo Scupoll. 1st Ed 1589

[17] Ejercicio de Perfección y Virtudes Cristianas. Venerable P. Alonso Rodríguez. 1st Ed 1609

[18] *Practice of love for Jesus Christ. Saint Alfose Liguori. 1st Ed circa 1750*

Examinations

Every person doing the exercises must examine his conscience at noon and at night about the faults he has committed in general and in particular in the rules of their exercises. But for the devout people for whom specifically I write this instruction, it is convenient for them to also do a practical examination on the state of their soul, on the desire to advance in virtue, or on the profit they derive from the Holy Sacraments, either in the way they make their mental prayer or the vocal prayers, or in dealing with their neighbor, or in the fulfillment of their obligations, the use they make of inspirations, and finally, checking a thousand inclinations and disorderly affections sometimes hidden to those who have them.

Since no one may want to amend what he does not know, and these slight inclinations and shortcomings are not so easily known, from this comes the usefulness of these examinations to direct the will to correctly trace in the exercises in their plan of amendment for the future.

To this end, it is not enough to get to know their bad inclinations; it is also convenient to look for their origin or their causes and to know the remedy. For example: find one who lies not once but continuously: one who is inclined to lie. Well, first of all examine how often you lie, then where the origin of this easiness to lie comes from. If it is for much talking, or for the indifference with which you look at the lie, or for the pleasure of attracting attention with extraordinary things, or for fear of looking bad, etc. If they lie at any time and in any place, or only in certain times or more frequent places. Knowing this, it is easy to determine the remedy by removing the causes, the occasion, the motive, etc.

In this way, the origin of all the other defects into which they fall frequently must be sought, since the mistakes that are committed once in a while do not form a habit, nor are they the object of these practical examinations, but rather those more frequent defects. And I will say that these exams can be done in a comfortable posture, such as sitting, walking, etc.

Mortification

Mortification is intended to unchain the spirit, so that the heart can better feel the motion of divine grace, in the same way as the retreat has indicated.

Mortification can be interior and exterior. The interior one is to grieve one of on past faults, and to restrain from the excesses of appetite and exercise of the will. The exterior consists of mortifications of the body, such as fasting, wearing cilices, using disciplines, etc. Internal mortification must be practiced by everyone. But for the exterior, each one must consult with his confessor, whose prudence assesses those that may be practiced. The same schedule of hours to get up, to lie down and for all the rest that the person involved in the exercises has to observe can also be seen as a mortification, and this everyone must practice it without fear and with constancy.

Vocal prayer

Finally, vocal prayer is also part of the exercises, such as visits to the Blessed Sacrament (which are highly recommended in such times),The Way of the Cross. Rosary, Mass, Little Office of Mary, etc.

The object of vocal prayer is, first: to draw abundant graces and to get much fruit out of the exercises; and second, to spend in a holy way part of the time, thus making the task of the whole day smoother. For this reason, no more vocal prayers should be said than those indicated by the director of the exercises, and in the way and manner prescribed by him, omitting the other devotions that he is used to do, in order not to interrupt the order followed on the exercises.

Q. According to this, should there be any order in these practices of prayer, reading and others that make up the exercises?

A. Without a doubt; and this is one of the most important things to do well.

Q, And what order is that?

R. You cannot set the same order for everyone, because that depends on the circumstances of the person, and so the schedule of hours that they must observe remains in the care of the director, and in which he must always keep in mind that first is to alternate the practices that require more effort, which are mental prayer and spiritual reading, with the lesser ones of vocal prayers and rest. Secondly, arranging the practices in such a way that there are some free times so that he can have times either for unforeseen occupations, or to make some notes or to prepare for a general confession, or to think about to reform his life, etc. In no way should the body or the spirit be overloaded with too many practices, that they do not leave time neither to rest, nor to think about what he does and wants to do in the future.

Q. Well, at least put a possible example of the distribution of one day of exercises.

R. Assuming that he is entirely free of occupations to do his exercises, and that he is a healthy person, it could be indicated to him in the manner indicated in Annex I.

Q. And if the person cannot be available all day, what will he do?

R. Take up the hours you have free in the most important practices, which are mental prayer and spiritual reading; if it could be done, distributing these meditations and readings between working hours, in the order we have set for people free of occupations. That is why they must not stop if they can hear the mass, or praying a part of the rosary, nor the exams, but they can hear the mass while he is doing the mental prayer, and the rosary and the exams while he is occupied in his tasks or other endeavors .

Q. And those people who can only count on a few short moments each day, will they be able to do exercises?

A. Because they live so absorbed in their jobs, it is in their best interest to do them more than any other person.

Q. Well, what are they to do?

R. To do with much recollection their labors, occupying their heart in the best possible way in the meditation that corresponds to each day, at the same time that with the body they are working for their boss or parents, or people whom they report to. And do not doubt that doing so in the moments they have to be able to dedicate them exclusively to the exercises, however short they may be, will bring out as much and perhaps more fruit than the people free of duties who have been employing the whole day on it; because God will see their good will, and will reward it, granting them all the graces together in those precious moments, what He is giving to others in small portions.

As happened to that saint lay brother, who is said to have spent the day begging for alms for the community, retiring to pray only in the short time he was left free, God favored him with many graces. And since he had obtained permission from the superior to stop begging for the city and dedicate himself more to meditating, he no longer felt those consolations and favors that he had previously experienced. And disappointed by his own experience, he asked to be returned to his former position of collecting alms, resigning himself with the short periods that this obligation left him free. These continued to be as profitable as before, in favor of the great care that he put into walking very recollected during the day, and almost meditating through the streets that he walked with his bag on his shoulder.

Q. How many days are there to be spent on the exercises?

A. Although Saint Ignatius indicates four weeks, which are to be completed in thirty days, he himself also put forth another shorter method of eight days. Thus commonly speaking it will suffice to use eight whole days, to which we will add the preparation to be done the night before, with which the holy exercises are already begun, and the conclusion the morning after the exercises, with which which come to be the same number of days that the Apostles used in the Upper Room.

Q. And at what times should the exercises be done?

A. There is no specific times for it, and everyone will see the time when they can do it with more ease. Some may imitate the Apostles, and they do them in the days that mediate between the Ascension of the Lord and the coming of the Holy Spirit. Others practice them in Advent, many in Lent, which seems preferable to me for two reasons. The first, because it is a time for prayer, mortification and solitude. The second, because Lent ends with Holy Week, in which the Church celebrates the death of our Lord Jesus Christ, the resolutions that the fear of death, judgment and hell formulated in the exercises will be corroborated again in Easter, and for a much more noble principle of love and gratitude to the goodness of the divine Redeemer, who in these festivities is considered to be suffering for men.

Q. *What else remains to be said in the matter?*

A. First. That in the exercises one must enter with much encouragement and great hope to derive abundant fruit from them. Second. That during the exercises one does not receive communion, and therefore does not go to confession; but there is never more need than then to go to the spiritual director to discover the muddy feelings of the heart, and to communicate the effects that the exercises produce in them, whether they are pleasures and consolations, whether they are dryness and sadness. Third. That the resolutions that are made, be written on paper, both so that they are not forgotten and to give them greater importance.

Q. *How about resolutions?*

A. The resolutions are those decisions that one takes to amend oneself in such and such a thing, as God has made known to them in prayer especially. For this knowledge, the practical exams that we said about one's inclinations also help a lot. If these exams have been done well, you will have an exact knowledge of the bad inclinations of our soul that are most in need of amendment, and the most effective remedies to cure them. This desire to apply the remedies forms the commitments that we call resolutions, and by which the fruit or benefit derived from the exercises is measured. It is not necessary that they be many, nor expressed with many words. But it will be convenient if they are the most appropriate to root out the bad habits or continued falls that we experience in ourselves: see what we said above about the exams.

Q. And when are the resolutions to be written?

A. The best time is the last day in the morning, especially if (as is customary in the town of Bilbao where this book is written), there is general communion on that day. In this way, not only will they be done correctly in the solemn moments in which the real presence of Jesus in the soul has just been tasted, but also the rest of that precious day remains to consolidate oneself in the fulfillment of what is resolved from the exercises. And what difficulties can stop him on such a day? On that day the fervor of the previous days serves as a preparation to receive the Author of grace, who comes in person to inspire them what they should do from now on to amend their life, and to give them strength to begin to implement what God himself has inspired them. Accordingly, it is clear that on the last day one should not occupy oneself in practical examinations, because his goal is already fulfilled.

Q. And are you not exercising for any reason other than the life amendment?

A Also for success in choosing a state of life.

Q. And in this case, how are they made?

R. As already indicated, with the variations that we are now going to say. After spending the first four or five days in the meditations of the Last Days, with practical exams to amend life, at the same time choosing a state of life; the next day, that is the fifth or the sixth, begins with the meditation of the Incarnation, and in the afternoon and at night it continues with that of the two flags, that of Jesus Christ and that of the devil. Instead of the practical examinations, one must think how among those who serve God. Some do so by abandoning the world, and following the evangelical counsels, and others without leaving the world, are satisfied just by observing God's precepts.

The next morning, the end for which we have been created is meditated on again; and once this meditation is over, the choice is made in one of two ways. First. One proposes the various states that they can embrace, and after trying to be as indifferent as possible to each of them, for which the meditation that has just been done will greatly help, they ask God to move them to what was more his divine pleasure. Immediately, the benefits and harms that may result to our soul from taking that state, and the benefits and failures from not taking it, are running through each of these two. Made this attempt in all the states, it is observed which of them their heart are inclined to, not by worldly or earthly liking, by passion that has been conceived or by their appetites, but by the opinion of the reason that has weighed all the consequences, and the goods and evils to be followed of either choice. And still to convince oneself better that the choice you have taken to such a state is by the exercise of reason and not by the human likes or dislikes, go again to prayer, and there expose to the Lord the choice you have made, and ask him to deign to confirm on it if it is to his liking, with the humble confidence that He will make known his divine will.

The second way to make the choice of the state of life is according to these four rules. Proposed the various states, and putting the heart in the greatest possible indifference, as has been said in the first way, one discerns if the love that moves them to choose comes from God, so that they know that the choice they do is solely for God. This is the 1st rule. 2nd, to take into consideration any man, and desiring for him all perfection, to consider what I would tell him to do to choose what is most pleasing to God and profitable to his soul. And this would serve for their own choice. 3rd, to place oneself at the moment of death, and make the choice according to what I think I would want then. 4th, putting myself on the day of judgment, and choose what I wanted then. Having made the choice on these four rules, go to prayer so that the Lord, as it was said in the first way, confirms the choice made, the exercises are followed until their conclusion. I finish this appendix, noting that the particular exam, which is supposed to be done by the people who read this, should be held in the first months after the exercises on the resolutions that have been taken in them, starting immediately after completing the exercises to preserve in full force those resolutions, and thus put them into effect rather than to cool down the fervor, which facilitates even difficult things.

Second Appendix

About different temperaments

Many and mixed are the thoughts that men have formed about the rich variety with which the Supreme Maker has distributed temperaments among us. Those who in our classification have been favored in the third and fifth, let us say so, are happy with their lot, and convinced that they are already virtuous without practicing virtue. At the same time those who have had the worst part, either hide with the rebellion of their temperament to remain in a guilty ignorance, or anguished desist from what they ardently desired and who see it as impossible to achieve. Every day they are repeating to themselves publicly: *I am not good for virtue; my temperament is not fit for those things: if I did not have this temperament...* and other expressions like that.

Having thus taught in this little book an easy and effective way of acquiring virtue, it was right to omit complaints that not only clumsily offend the goodness of our God, but also promote leisure in the ways of the Lord, fortify the inclination towards evil, and weaken the healthy desires for good. First of all, it is a fact that there are some temperaments so well disposed, so friendly to serve and to please, who steal hearts, and make a place for themselves everywhere; and others, on the contrary, as if the curse of God had fallen upon them, offer us nothing but reasons for continued displeasure, both in the civil and in the religious areas.

However, this difference is not as huge as it appears at first glance; because there are no temperaments, as good as they are, that lack any flaw nor so bad that they do not have some good traits. And anyway, whether you look at temperaments due to physical complexions, or as the inclination of the will impregnated with Adam's sin, it is only a natural principle and natural principles mean nothing in the supernatural order.

It is true that the ways of nature, and much more those of grace, are for us a mystery whose dense veil we are not allowed to unravel. But before the great darkness that forms this veil, we have a shining light that makes these words very readable: *You are the cause of your perdition, Israel; I have done nothing but give you the help you had.* Thus speaks a God of goodness, a loving Father, who in spite of the upheaval caused in us by the first disobedience, looks at us tenderly and does not want anyone to perish but all to live eternally.

So what! Would the generous hand of the Savior have imprinted upon those endowed with evil character the fatal seal of reprobation? Have these not been sprinkled like all the others with the blood of the Lamb? Ah! if we were to count only on our own efforts, surely one would have a great advantage over the others. But no: the Lord who disregards no one with the help of his grace, and who is faithful not to allow our temptations to be greater than our forces, will take care to provide each one according to his needs.

I would distinguish among bad temperaments two kinds of evil: the corruption of habit and that of nature. I'll explain myself.

There are apparently very crooked and evil-inclined characters; because education, bad companies and many other causes have transformed them into the defects of the objects to which they have been directed; and such temperaments, to be very praiseworthy do only need being presented with objects worthy of praise.

In Magdalene and in Paul we have two beautiful examples of this truth. Magdalene was a very loving temperament; led by this propensity, she had herself to be dragged into vice, and she became a despicable woman in the most necessary garment for those of her sex. The Savior touched her heart, and in the move that grace worked in her, she left her temperament intact. The one who had been a lover before her conversion, was also a lover afterwards, but lover not of those objects with whom she lost her innocence, but of the one who helped her to recover it. And Magdalene remained in love the rest of her life, but in love with Jesus Christ.

Paul had a fiery temperament. Active, a doer; and his temperament before grace changed him, developed perversely, to persecuting the Church of the Lord. The hand of God struck him on the road to Damascus, and from this moment the object of his temperament was changed, but his temperament itself didn't; the one who was a doer before, was a doer also after; but his undertakings were no longer aimed at persecuting and destroying the nascent religion, but at preserving and propagating it.

Do you see how grace sweetly and wisely directs nature, and makes the virtues sprout in our hearts like flowers that the earth spontaneously produced? The maxims of the world that we have formed, these are really incompatible with virtue and can never be twinned with it or compromised in their claims; but the natural can subsist, accommodating grace in a certain way to our weakness, to make the practice of virtue easier and more pleasant.

These temperaments of which I have just spoken are improperly called bad; but there are others who have such deep-rooted corruption that they can be properly said: that in retirement, in dealing with people, in any circumstances, they are always unbearable to themselves, and unbearable also to others. Ahead of them they carry haste and violence in all their actions, and behind them they leave regrets and regrets without number, communicating to all who touch the bitterness of their harshness. People of this class never succeed in blaming their evil for what they do, but blame their own temperament, and not infrequently that of others. In their judgment, all their outbursts and virulent ways come from the temperament of others or from the circumstances in which they find themselves, and which in their opinion were just enough to try the patience of the most patient man.

It is true that these people have to do violence to themselves to conform to the rules of sweetness that the Gospel prescribes; But is this an impossible thing? On the contrary, the Lord wanted to do with such ostentation of greater mercy, allowing more obstacles in them to give rise to more brilliant and multiplied successes. Far from such temperaments being inept for virtue, none are more capable of constancy or greatness. The task is arduous, I confess, but grace is ready and it can accomplish everything.

And although this work produced no other advantage than making society and human dealings welcome, it would be an imponderable asset to reform one's temperament, and to know how to mold it to that of others. What more beautiful thing than dealing with people who always have peace on their lips, without the strong winds of a whimsical, violent and raptured temperament ever raising waves of anger and turbulent expressions? This single effect caused by grace is indisputable proof that virtue makes our luck bearable in this country of misfortunes, and that even if it was not the way to heaven, men should seek it as a resting place on the Earth.

Only remains to say two words to those of natural sweet and peaceful temperament.

Satisfied are the people who have this imaginary treasure, made the object of constant envy by those who think they are less fortunate, because they need more effort and fatigue to get to where they have arrived without much pain or work. However, those that by nature have a peaceful temperament have no less need of cultivation than the rebels. The proposition will seem strange to some, but I will demonstrate it with specific evidence.

A peaceful temperament easily accommodates to others, wants to leave no one unhappy, and sometimes sacrifices his comfort to please everyone. But this very propensity so worthy of appreciation and praise is exposed to two great drawbacks. First: to degenerate the dear sweetness into guilty condescension; because the inclination easily transcends the just limits, and by following some inspirations that were always believed innocent, the crime is sometimes approved, and it is also possible to cooperate to consummate it. This fact exists, and it is not necessary for me to stop to test him, since even the least insightful views can see it; but the bitter fruits that a false sweetness produces, start in us a sad woe! that comes from the depths of the heart.

The second drawback is that it can be corrupted more easily, and this is a natural consequence of what I have just said. A flexible temperament equally bends to the right as to the left; and if it is enviable when in the hands of grace it rises to form a leafy tree, it is very worthy of pity when malice twists and bends it towards the vices of the people whose advice of iniquity they allow themselves to be seduced. And if is as easy for virtue as for vice, inconstancy in the ways of God is the result of a good temperament if he does not take care to cultivate it carefully.

Added to all this is the danger of confusing the operations of nature with those of grace, attributing to it what was the work of their own inclination and their whim. And in this case, what merit can have in the divine presence deeds produced by a purely natural goodness and similar to those of a faithful or a heretic, whose good works have no more than not being bad? What will be worthy actions performed with pleasure, yes, and with pleasure, but scorched at the very root with mortal guilt? And even when they are in the happy state of innocence, is it not a pity to have idle the grace they had been given to perfect operations that led them by hand to the path of justice and holiness?

So let us give glory to God; Let us vindicate his wise and beneficial Providence in the uneven distribution of temperaments; Let's say full of joy that everyone, everyone, whatever they may be, can be directed to virtue. It remains, indelible in us, that temperament is a natural principle. That of all supernatural operations, the only ones worthy of merit are due exclusively to grace; and that if the latter is more favorable to virtue than others, these disadvantages are compensated with other benefits. And that if Providence has wished to show off its fruitfulness in so many and so diverse temperaments, it will also make it show the efficacy of its power, when admitted to the vision of the divine Essence, it makes us see in it the admirable and hidden paths where he has led his creatures to the heavenly homeland. The study of our temperament and the effort to reform it are the consequences that we must draw from this consoling truth that I have just laid down.

Saint Augustine has stated that everything that is wrong and sinful in our words, our actions and our thoughts, entails its origin in the malice of our nature. The passions and affections of the soul are like the germs and the common matter of all the vices and of all the virtues. Thus speaks this apostolic Father, thus speak those who have deepened the human heart, thus speaks our own experience. We find for some easier to fall into anger, others into impurity, these for leisure, those for work; and these differences are not born from any other cause than from the different impressions that temperaments receive from the passions that is more sympathetic with it.

The same principle recognizes that strange amalgam of vices and virtues that we notice in some people. The stamp of the temperament itself is engraved in all their actions, and this is why they miss the constancy with which grace wants us to walk towards the end that we should always aim for in our good works. When grace operates, man behaves ordinarily and does everything for God: nothing for the world, everything for the spirit, nothing for the flesh. But when the temperament gives to its impulses, sometimes what is built with one hand is destroyed with the other. And judging by the facts, we will not know who to please: whether the author of the virtues that were practiced in the morning, or the one of the vices that he allowed to be carried away in the afternoon.

It is, therefore, an occupation of the utmost importance for man to investigate the root cause of his most frequent defects, and to remedy them with his desire for conversion. This reform of the heart is demanded of us by religion, and it itself provides us with the means to achieve it. But not only religion: society and our own state demand of us this most useful task.

In His admirable dispositions God has made man a social animal, has given each one their peculiar character, so that from all individuals a compact whole is formed, in which one needs the other and thus strengthens their relations with the various trades that each one following their inclination lend each other. But this diversity of characters inevitably produces the opposition of temperaments, which sometimes makes human relationships very annoying.

We have met a talkative person, who intends to usurp the right of others to the precious gift of the word in conversation. Or with another austere, somber and meditative person, who with their silent temperament seems to censor our joyful disposition. Here the unfounded apprehensions of a suspicious and distrusting temperament torment ours, simply and straightforwardly; there is the phlegmatic nature of those who live with us and that is in continuous conflict with our temperament, that is alive and burning. Not even the closest links of flesh and blood are enough to remedy this continuing opposition. For how can we preserve in society the enchanting peace with ourselves, and the much appreciated harmony with our fellow men? There is no other way than by reforming our natural inclinations, and making them flexible enough to accommodate the various moldings of other people's temperaments.

And not only does this unpleasant opposition result from the variety of temperaments, but also from the kind of occupations to which one has to devote oneself vey choice or by force in one's own state of life or employment. How many very repugnant roles to their nature don't need the men forced to represent in society? How many positions, how many jobs, how many businesses that are in open contradiction to their natural inclination? It is therefore necessary to engage in this interesting task that takes our imperfections at the root, makes society sweet and makes any kind of work bearable.

A story to end with

But is it advisable to avoid as much as possible the treatment of badly conditioned temperaments, or rather to seek them with determination to better rid ourselves with their continuous blows? Fleeing when choice is in our hands is an effective but momentary remedy, which leaves intact all the bitter hostility of our temperament, and all its vigor for another occasion when escape is not possible. Self-love will never lack specious pretexts to defend this measure, which can only be adopted with weak spirits with whom palliative remedies must be used because they refuse radical cures. This was the opinion of Saint Anthony in the consultation that a solitary saint made with him, in the difficulty he felt of suffering a character so malignant and difficult to get along with, that I have found it worthy to finish this Appendix with his history, to serve as a model and edification to those who have to deal with bad people.

"Traveling this holy man, he found on the way a poor man, hurt, covered in sores and unable to take a step to beg for his livelihood. Moved with compassion, he took him to his cell, helped him as much as he could, and after some time he convalesced, invited him to stay with him forever. The poor man gladly accepted this offer, which in order to be fulfilled by the servant of God, had to redouble his activity if he were to achieve the fruit of their labor for both of them.

"It didn't take the poor man many days to complain that he was feeding him poorly, even though he had treated him better than himself. To the complaints he later added insults; and although he was ashamed of the patience with which his benefactor suffered them, he asked for forgiveness, he quickly returned to his fury, conceiving against him such mortal hatred that he said to him: *I do not want to live with you; take me back to the path where you found me, that I'm not used to being so poorly fed.*

"The loner asked for forgiveness, promising that he would strive to give him a better deal from now on. To this end, it occurred to him to go to the hut of a neighbor shepherd, who offered to give him some food every day. With this the poor man seemed content; but after a few weeks he began to say to him: *Rascal, you are a hypocrite: you play the role of asking for alms to feed me, and it is for you: you eat the best things alone, and you give me the leftovers.*

"*Ah! My brother*, the loner replied, *you do me wrong: I assure you that I ask nothing for myself: if you are not happy with my services, have at least patience for the love of Jesus Christ, and hope that I will behave better.*

"*I do not need your warnings,*" replied the poor man; and taking a stone, he threw it to his benefactor's head, who could avoid this blow, but not that of a club with which he immediately shook him, making him fall to the ground with the violence with which he unloaded him: *"God forgive you"*, he said the lonely, *"that I have already forgiven you"*.

"*Yes,*" replied the poor man, "*you tell me that you forgive me, but only with your lips; what you want is to see me dead"*. The benefactor assured him of his good affection, and was still going to hug him as a sign of reconciliation; but the poor man grabbed him by the throat, ripped his whole face with his fingernails, and tried to drown him.

"Three years the servant of God continued with him in this way, the cruelties that he had to suffer from him were unspeakable, in addition to his continuous insults and foolish sayings, that he should returned him to the place where he had picked him up, and that he wanted more to starve or thirst, or be devoured by beasts, than live with him. At the end of this time, he was doubtful about the party he was going to take, because if he returned to the road, as the poor man wanted with repeated instances or supplications, he feared that he would perish from misery, and otherwise he was also afraid of losing patience with him. He went to consult the great Antonio. The Saint spoke to him as an inspired man of God in these terms: *"Ah! my son: be careful, that the thought you have of separating yourself from that poor man is a temptation of the devil, who tries to take off your crown. If you abandon him, God will not abandon him"*.

"But, my Father," replied the lonely young man, *"I fear I will lose my patience with him"*.

"And why will you lose it?" Replied the Saint, *"do you not know that we must exercise charity more generously with those who do us the most harm? What merit would you have in being patient with a person who did not contradict you, or make you suffer any evil? Do you not know that charity is a generous virtue, that does not look at the vices of the one who afflicts us, but at God, and only at God? So, my son, keep that poor man with you, and in proportion to his wickedness use compassion on him. Whatever you do out of charity, Jesus Christ will receive it as done to his person. Show with your patience that you are a disciple of a patient God, and remember that this virtue and that of charity make the Christian known. Look at this poor man as the means that God uses to craft your crown"*.

"The host man followed the advice of Saint Anthony, and he treated the poor with more charity than before. God blessed his undeifeated patience. And he had the consolation of seeing the poor man finally converted, and spending the rest of his days in penance and sanctity of life. "

103

Anexes

I. *Possible schedule for full-time exercises.*

At 5 am. Get up and thank God.

From 5 1/2 to 6 1/2. The 1st hour of mental prayer.

From 6 1/2 to 6 3/4. Think about how you have behaved in prayer, feelings you have experienced and so on.

From 6 3/4 to 7 1/4. Mass and station to the Blessed Sacrament.

From 7 1/4 to 7 3/4. The 1st spiritual reading.

From 7 3/4 to 8 1/2. Breakfast, rest and free time.

From 8 1/2 to 9. The hours of the Breviary or 1st part of the Rosary.

From 9 to 10. The 2nd hour of mental prayer.

From 10 to 10 1/2. Think about how it has gone in prayer and rest.

From 10 to 10 1/2. Practical exam and free time.

From 11 1/2 to 12 pm. The 2nd spiritual reading.

From 12 to 1. The Via-Crucis and particular exam of the day.

From 1 to 3. Lunch and rest.

From 3 to 3 1/4. The Breviary or the 2nd part of the rosary with the visit to the Blessed Sacrament.

From 3 3/4 to 4 1/2. Mental prayer, and think about how it went for you.

From 4 1/2 to 5 1/2. Silent walk.

From 5 1/2 to 6. The 3rd spiritual reading.

From 6 to 6 1/2. The 3rd part of the rosary with some short prayers.

From 6 1/2 to 7 1/2. The 4th hour of mental prayer.

From 7 1/2 to 8. Think about how your prayer has been, and free time.

From 8 to 8 1/2. The 4th spiritual reading.

From 8 1/2 to 9 1/2. Dinner and rest.

From 9 1/2 to 10. General examination of the faults, with the particular about the way in went on the distribution of the day, and going to bed.

II. Tables to keep the accounting of the faults.

Its use is as follows:

Knowing the number of fouls in which one has fallen since the previous examination, the corresponding number is searched in table 1, and the peak in which the number is is doubled. In the following exam, the faults of the two exams are combined, and doubling the peak in which the faults had been recorded the previous day, the corresponding to the sum of faults of the two exams is doubled, taking care at the same time to compare the faults, and recognize on which of the days there have been the greatest number of them. In this way it continues until the day of confession. Then the faults in the 1st table are passed to the 1st confession in the 2nd table; beginning in that new account, which will end on the day of the next confession, in which the faults will be passed to the 2nd confession in the 2nd table; and in this order it continues until the end of the month in which the faults of all the confessions will be gathered, and will be noted in the 3rd table.

Warning:

In order not to make this booklet too bulky, the following tables have been made so small that the first and third tables only contain two columns of nine numbers each, and the second one only, since each sheet of said table serves two confessions, as can be seen with a simple glance over all of them. However, the faults and the times that the acts have been omitted on the proposed virtue, (which for that is the second box in all the columns) can be recorded with the utmost accuracy, raising two or more numbers as necessary: Namely if there are 13 fouls, this number cannot be found; then double the 10 and the 3. They are 124, there is not; but it is achieved by raising 80, 40 and 4; and so any other else. (Editor Note: the author assumes in the readers the practice of confession with weekly frequency).

First Table

For daily exams

Faults	Omitted Acts		Faults	Omitted Acts
1	1		10	10
2	2		12	12
3	3		14	14
4	4		16	16
5	5		18	18
6	6		20	20
7	7		40	40
8	8		60	60
9	9		80	80

Second Table (1)

Destined for the faults of each confession.

First Confession			Second Confession	
Faults	Omitted Acts		Faults	Omitted Acts
1	1		1	1
2	2		2	2
3	3		3	3
4	4		4	4
5	5		5	5
10	10		10	10
20	20		20	20
40	40		40	40
80	80		80	80

Second Table (2)

Destined for the faults of each confession.

Third Confession			Fourth Confession	
Faults	Omitted Acts		Faults	Omitted Acts
1	1		1	1
2	2		2	2
3	3		3	3
4	4		4	4
5	5		5	5
10	10		10	10
20	20		20	20
40	40		40	40
80	80		80	80

Second Table (3)

Destined for the faults of each confession.

Fifth Confession			Sixth Confession	
Faults	Omitted Acts		Faults	Omitted Acts
1	1		1	1
2	2		2	2
3	3		3	3
4	4		4	4
5	5		5	5
10	10		10	10
20	20		20	20
40	40		40	40
80	80		80	80

Second Table (4)

Destined for the faults of each confession.

Seventh Confession			Eighth Confession	
Faults	Omitted Acts		Faults	Omitted Acts
1	1		1	1
2	2		2	2
3	3		3	3
4	4		4	4
5	5		5	5
10	10		10	10
20	20		20	20
40	40		40	40
80	80		80	80

Third Table

Intended for all-month fouls

Faults	Omitted Acts		Faults	Omitted Acts
1	1		50	50
2	2		100	100
3	3		200	200
4	4		300	300
5	5		400	400
10	10		500	500
20	20		600	600
30	30		700	700
40	40		800	800